Penguin Books

P9-DEN-419

The End of the Road

John Margolies is a photographer, lecturer, and critic whose special interest is vernacular architecture and popular culture. Major exhibitions of his architectural photographs include "Morris Lapidus: Architecture of Joy," shown at the Architectural League of New York, and "Resorts of the Catskills," shown at the Cooper-Hewitt Museum, New York City. The first traveling exhibition of his photographs was mounted this year by The Hudson River Museum: "The End of the Road: 20th Century Commercial Architecture in the U.S." His work has been published in national magazines and professional journals, including The New York Times Magazine, Esquire, and Progressive Architecture. His projects have been funded by sources such as the Guggenheim Foundation, the New York State Council on the Arts, and the National Endowment for the Arts. When not traveling the length and breadth of the United States, John Margolies lives in New York City.

The End of the Road

Photographs and Text by

John Margolies

Edited by C. Ray Smith
Designed by Ivan Chermayeff

Penguin Books
in collaboration with The Hudson River Museum

Exhibition circulated by Independent Curators Incorporated, New York

Penguin Books Ltd, Harmondsworth,
Middlesex, England
Penguin Books, 625 Madison Avenue,
New York, New York 10022, U.S.A.
Penguin Books Australia Ltd, Ringwood,
Victoria, Australia
Penguin Books Canada Limited, 2801 John Street,
Markham, Ontario, Canada L3R 1B4
Penguin Books (N.Z.) Ltd, 182—190 Wairau Road,
Auckland 10, New Zealand

First published in the United States of America
in simultaneous hardcover and paperback editions
by The Viking Press (A Studio Book) and Penguin Books 1981

LIBRARY OF CONGRESS CATALOGING IN PUBLICATION DATA
Margolies, John S
   The end of the road.
   1.   Photography, Architectural.   2.   United
States—Description and travel—Views.   I.   Smith,
C. Ray.   II.   Hudson River Museum.   III.   Title.
TR659.M37   1981b   779'.9917304925   80-39907
ISBN 0 14 00.5840 0

Printed in the United States of America
Set in Trade Gothic Condensed Bold and Franklin Gothic

Acknowledgments

On behalf of the Board of Trustees and staff of The Hudson River Museum, I want to express my sincere appreciation to John Margolies, who has worked diligently and enthusiastically on this project which involved two research trips across the country, including travel to states from Oregon, California, and Montana, to Texas, New Mexico, and Alabama, to Florida, Delaware, and New Jersey. This photographic survey was conducted under the auspices of The Hudson River Museum, with a matching grant from the Visual Arts Program of the National Endowment for the Arts.

I am especially grateful to Mary Wachs of Viking Penguin for her commitment to this project and for her concern for the quality of this publication, which The Hudson River Museum has co-published with Viking Penguin.

Special thanks are due Ivan Chermayeff and his assistant, George Shakespear, for their outstanding design of the catalogue, invitation, and exhibition installation, and to C. Ray Smith, who worked closely with John Margolies on the editing of the catalogue manuscript.

I express my gratitude to Joan K. Davidson, Kathy Gauss, Catherine Conn, Mrs. Robert S. Siffert, Joseph DeBlasi, Coco Eiseman, Peter Blake, Robert Venturi, John Morris Dixon, Howard Gilman, and Suzanne Davis for their encouragement and support of this project.

I acknowledge with thanks the many members of The Hudson River Museum who worked on facets of the exhibition: Julie Brown, Associate Curator, who assisted in the organization and preparation of the catalogue and the exhibition; Julie Lazar, Director of Development, and her assistant, Judith Richards, who provided crucial support in all aspects of the project; Richard B. Carlson, who was responsible for administrative details related to the survey and the exhibition; Barbara Hammond, Registrar; Mary Krall, who patiently and carefully transcribed the manuscripts from tape; John Holmes and Jeff Casper, who skillfully handled the task of installation; Nancy Hoyt, Curator of Education, and her assistant, Maryann Strebel; and Tom Finkelpearl, Coordinator of Public Relations. To these staff members and to others who collaborated on this exhibition, I express my gratitude.

This exhibition is made possible, in part, with public funds from the National Endowment for the Arts, a federal agency in Washington, D.C., and the New York State Council on the Arts. Private funding was provided by the J. M. Kaplan Fund, The Gilman Paper Company, Philip Johnson, Carolyn Marsh, Barbara Jakobson, and the members of The Hudson River Museum.

Richard Koshalek
Director, The Hudson River Museum

Air France
AMAX Foundation, Inc.
American Can Company Foundation
American Express Company
American Philanthropic Foundation
Mr. Andrew J. Balint
The Bank of New York—County Trust
   Region
Bell & Stanton, Inc.
Mr. Edwin L. Bilby
Mr. Baldo Castelli
Chemical Bank
Chubb & Son, Inc.
CIBA-GEIGY Corporation
Citibank, N. A.
Mr. & Mrs. Saul Z. Cohen
Consolidated Edison Co. of N.Y.
Miss Anne Dayton
Mr. Joseph DeBlasi
Dr. Charles DeCarlo
Gannett Newspaper Foundation
General Foods Corporation
Gestetner Corporation
Gilman Paper Company
GK Technologies, Inc.
Dr. & Mrs. Leonard M. Greene
Mr. & Mrs. Gregory Halpern
The Hudson River Museum Auxiliary

The Hudson River Museum Foundation
Hudson Valley National Bank
IBM Corporation
Industrial Solvents Corporation
Mr. Philip Johnson
The J. M. Kaplan Fund, Inc.
Mr. Donald R. Klein
Mr. Thomas J. Langan, Jr.
Laurel Printing, Inc.
Howard & Jean Lipman Foundation
Ms. Carolyn Marsh
Media Networks, Inc.
Mr. & Mrs. Tristram W. Metcalfe, Jr.
Mobil Foundation, Inc.
National Bank of North America
National Endowment for the Arts
National Endowment for the
   Humanities
New York State Council on the Arts
New York Telephone Company
Mrs. Barbara Newington
Otis Elevator Company
H. M. Pack Foundation
Peoples Westchester Savings Bank
PepsiCo, Inc.
Polychrome Corporation
Precision Valve Corporation
Sarah I. Schieffelin Residuary Trust

Scientific American, Inc.
Mrs. Robert S. Siffert
Dr. & Mrs. Norman Simon
Mr. Frederick J. Stock
The Surdna Foundation
Texaco, Inc.
Dr. Charles C. Tillinghast, Jr.
Mrs. Oliver J. Troster
Union Carbide Corporation
Wells, Rich, Greene, Inc.
The Westchester Community
   Foundation
Westchester County
Lorraine Wild
City of Yonkers
Xerox Corporation
Anonymous

Special thanks to: Richard Koshalek, Director of The Hudson River Museum, for making the book and exhibition happen; Julie Brown, Julie Lazar and the staff of The Hudson River Museum; C. Ray Smith, for assembling the text from transcripts of my interviews and lectures; Mary Wachs of Penguin Books, an editor extraordinaire; Ivan Chermayeff, for his vision and design; and Maxene Fabe, for interviewing and encouraging me; the helpful and friendly proprietors of the many commercial establishments who supplied me with information, moved cars, and otherwise assisted me; the local and regional specialists—architects, historians, educators, students, and preservationists—who shared their expertise with me; Philip Johnson, for his many insights; the John Simon Guggenheim Memorial Foundation; the Design Arts and Visual Arts Programs of the National Endowment for the Arts in Washington, D.C., a federal agency; and the New York State Council on the Arts, for supporting my work; Billy Adler, Barbara Jakobson, Ethel Margolies, Carolyn Marsh, and Stephen Resnick, for standing behind me, sometimes even to the point of propping me up; Bob Jensen, Bobbie Fisher, and Suzanne Stephens, for cat-sitting above and beyond the call of duty; and the Artex company for its collapsible bedboard made of pressed multi-fiber wood pulp.

John Margolies
New York City
September 1980

Driving on any road can be an adventure; it's like being an explorer. Just put me behind the wheel, preferably going nowhere, and I become Christopher Columbus—in Arkansas. At any turn there's the chance of coming on something that is extraordinary and absolutely amazing—a gas station, a diner, an old motel, or a "roadside attraction." As far as I am concerned, those places where you have to go 35 mph, with stoplights and people turning onto and off the road, and billboards screaming for attention, display the pulse of America's creative, native spirit.

For the past five years I have traveled the road photographing the best of whatever has survived from the seven decades of American road life. It has been an odyssey across the forty-eight contiguous United States—some one hundred thousand miles—and it has resulted in a unique record—approximately fifteen thousand slides—of the artifacts of the American roadside environment.

What I photograph is the outsides of things as seen from the road, the facades that promise adventures within. I am interested in the stylistic quirks, in what things look like at a glance as representations of what they are.

Most of my pictures are taken along the strips between small cities and towns—those highways that used to be the main drags. That is where this kind of architecture has survived best. It can be found in out-of-the-way places, old secondary roads, and in cities where growth came to a halt. Big, growing, vital cities usually destroy their commercial vernacular too quickly, so I generally avoid them in my search.

I can remember the agony of the family vacation, driving out in the family car as a kid and never stopping at places you thought were terrific. Taking a car trip was a tremendous adventure, a series of discoveries; it was an extension of your view of the world. The road was the new frontier. It had castles where you could get hot dogs and hamburgers, and places with believe-it-or-not things to see. Occasionally you stopped for gas at great mechanistic buildings where the gas pump gauges spun round hypnotically while mysterious investigations went on under the hood. But that was the only kind of stop you made.

You went whizzing by shiny railroad-car-like diners, past whole villages of Indian tepees where you could have spent the night, missing bright roadside attractions flapping with colorful pennants and flags, being tantalized all along the way by billboards and signs inviting, urging, insisting that you stop. The excitement and the disappointment at the same time—driving all the way from Ohio to Maine without stopping for ice cream at a Howard Johnson's, all the way from Texas to California without ever visiting an Indian trading post. Parents only wanted to get to the end of the road.

But it was that array of temptations that made any car trip exciting—these were the real ends of the road. It was America's twentieth-century Grand Tour. It was the Pilgrim's Progress—life as a journey set out on the road. And twentieth-century America developed a new form of that journey, with its heroic escapes and exasperating delays, its frolicsome fun and delicious escapades.

My earliest memory of the roadside from when I was a kid is the infamous Berlin Turnpike south of Hartford, Connecticut, now long since bypassed and crumbling. After a couple of hours of expressways, you suddenly came upon five miles of traffic lights and a 35-mph speed limit. The environment was all honky-tonk—gas-war gas stations, diners, drive-in movies, and motels. I later learned that it was known as Gasoline Alley because it was a tankful away from New York on the way to Boston. This five miles of stop-and-go was the highlight of any trip for me.

So it was only natural that the thirty days before my sixteenth birthday, when I could get my first driver's license, were the longest days of my life. It was the end of being cooped up and controlled. I had worked in awful jobs saving up money, and the minute I was sixteen I got a 1948 Oldsmobile 76 convertible. It was yellow; it was a wretched color. Once behind the wheel I started cruising to those places that I had been driven by before without stopping. Now I could stop.

I drove down to a cluster of roadside buildings in Darien, Connecticut, right near the Norwalk line, on Route 1. One place was called Cook's, which had been a Howard Johnson's and was converted into a hangout with pinball machines and tuna-fish sandwiches. Across the street were a Carvel's soft ice cream, a miniature golf course, and a gas station. What more could anyone need? I loved those kinds of places.

When I went to college they said, "No, all that is unimportant." And for about ten years I was taught that High Culture was better than low culture, that good taste is better than bad taste. Somehow the Judeo-Christian ethic seems to be "Like what you don't like and don't like what you do like." We were taught the opposite of the way things actually were. I was constantly being told to unlearn what I felt. So I lost touch with my suburban reality. It was intellectualized out of me.

Then in the late 1960s I began to reevaluate all of that. I cut through the years of pretension and made clear what my feelings were. I came back to terms with the person I was underneath all those layers of education, advice, and values. I began to reaffirm the values I had had as a child. I recognized that my past wasn't going to go away, that in fact within my past lay my future. I was finally able to go back, to look and learn from it. I began to rediscover what was left of my childhood fascinations.

By 1970 I had begun to make public assertions about the importance of vernacular architecture. Roadside architecture—the gas stations, motels, diners, and attractions that are represented and discussed in this book—is really about making people happy and serving their tastes rather than imposing values upon them. Professional architects and planners tried to impose an intellectual order upon the environment—at the expense of ornament, humor, and spontaneity. And they flushed the roadside environment down the drain. The symbolic and representational elements in architecture and design were obliterated by people who had assumed that they knew better than we did about what we wanted. What these people didn't understand was that they were also eliminating the soul, character, and individuality. It turns out that many untrained designers have a greater insight into what people would notice out of their car windows, and what will make them stop and buy.

The commercial architecture by the side of the road is very important; it is America's definitive contribution to the art of design in the twentieth century. It is not "that awful commercial garbage" that our parents hated so much; it is not blight and ugliness and bad taste. It proves that what we are really best at is being tacky and commercial. American capitalism manifested itself on the road with statements expressing pride in product. The small commercial business person was saying, "Here, look at me," and expressing this in buildings and signs.

This is splendid, wonderful folk architecture, and it is inventive and original. Most of us are in touch with memories of all those ticky-tacky roadside stands. I'm concerned with the average, everyday, run-of-the-mill experience rather than the special elevated experience. That is what I value most. That is what most everything is. But the majority of people have the opposite view. They tend to assign greater value to the unique and the monumental, ignoring the importance of our everyday experience— what we share in common.

Seven Decades of the Road Life

Without question the automobile has profoundly changed the physical environment and the ways in which we perceive our country. The automobile has transformed America from a series of rural enclaves into today's sophisticated, integrated, and unified system of transportation and communications. Driving is the spirit of freedom to explore this system, the spirit of movement through space.

Three developments led to America's automobile mania. It all began in 1903 with the first major oil strike in Beaumont, Texas, at the Spindletop Oil Field. Previously, when they were refining for kerosene (which was a superior substitute for whale oil since it didn't flicker when burning in a lamp) they also got this substance called gasoline, which they didn't know what to do with. So they threw it out. But soon the production of gasoline surpassed that of kerosene, although you still occasionally come across a kerosene pump in rural America. The Spindletop Motel sign (photograph 109), which is the only thing left of the motel, is shaped like an oil well to commemorate that Beaumont oil strike.

The second development was Henry Ford's production, in 1907, of the Model T that everyman could afford. And the third was the use of the glop left over from the oil refining process to make asphalt, which paved the roads for these new cars. These three converged by 1910 and set the pattern that held for seven delirious decades.

1910–1920: The first period in the history of roadside development goes from the beginning of the automobile to the beginning of the 1920s. With the automobile appeared the first architecture and facilities for this new life along the American road. Of these we know almost nothing except from old photographs, for the lifespan of buildings along the road was never great.

1920–1955: Around 1920, the Golden Age began. That first major change in scale of the roadside environment occurred when everyman could have a car and get on the road; it lasted until World War II introduced gasoline rationing. During that time more and more people started moving West. And some stopped along the way and opened up diners and gas stations. These are the mom-and-pop businesses of the thirties and forties that we are so nostalgic about today. They were strung out along the road at destinations determined by how long it took to drive from breakfasttime till you wanted lunch, and how long it took to drive in a day till you wanted sleep. Then, too, the national gas companies began to spread their design programs across the country, first regionally, then nationally. It was a slower time, not too long ago, when life moved at 35 mph.

1955–1973: In the mid 1950s, three new developments began to change the scale and appearance of the roadside environment dramatically: the advent of television; the corporate chains with their motel, gas station, and restaurant franchises; and the interstate highway system, which fostered a phase of corporate expansion that would forever alter the road as we had experienced it.

The improvement of highway design, along with the growth of leisure time and the carefully promoted concept of vacations, elevated automobile travel to new heights. People flocked by the carload to discover what was at the ends of American roads. Whereas in 1945 there were 31 million motor vehicles traveling some 250 billion vehicle miles, by 1960 more than twice that many cars were traveling some 718 billion miles.

Television and mass communications began to meld the country into an even smaller and more accessible area, by creating and reinforcing nationwide images of comfort, convenience, and reliability.

Huge, ubiquitous national concerns began to appear: Holiday Inns in 1953, McDonald's in 1955, and other conglomerates. Corporations learned that if they wanted to draw people off the road, they had to promote a strong, single image. If they were going to have one motel that was shaped like a tepee, the next one shouldn't be shaped like the Alamo or a goldfish.

Soon, a whole new set of faster roads—the interstate highways—tightened the massive campaign to standardize America. The interstates, ostensibly designed to expedite the evacuation of our cities in case of emergency, were built at a time of landscape "beautification," carrying with them the restriction that nothing could be built within six hundred feet of the highway.

The interstates brought new changes. First, they bypassed the towns and the previous commercial strips, depriving them of patrons who, moving at the new 60- and 70-mph speeds, were loath to get off their fast roads for any appreciable distance. Dick's Motor Inn in Banning, California (photograph 104), would have been an effective draw with its shocking-pink walls, except that, bypassed by the new highway, it was completely out of sight.

Second, the new six-hundred-foot restriction influenced the style and positioning of architecture that would be built near the interstate interchanges. Because signs were all you could see from the new roads, they became one-hundred-foot-high announcements to be seen at greater distances and speeds. Buildings became nearly identical. It no longer mattered how they appeared: their essence was conveyed by other means, and the message, reiterated all along the highways, was conformity and familiarity. McDonald's raised its golden parabolas and it was clear that corporate enterprise had congealed the roadside experience into a homogenized nationwide uniformity.

Homespun graphic symbols were eliminated. They were abstracted. The Flying Red Horse came down off the Mobil sign. Bolder and simpler designs replaced the richness of regional variety in this decline-by-franchise decade.

1973–1980: But in the 1970s began the series of gasoline shortages, recessions, and depressions that predicted the end of it all—the end of gasoline, of automobile travel, and ultimately, it seemed, the end of roadside architecture. The announcement of that death may be, as Mark

Twain said, somewhat exaggerated. But it caught us up short to what we had experienced, and what we might soon be missing. Now in the 1980s much of the roadside environment has already been destroyed, and all of it is threatened. This picture survey of gas stations, motels, food stops, and roadside attractions commemorates an America that is fast disappearing.

Gas: Pump and Circumstance

Gas stations are the most visited commercial buildings in the United States aside from food stores. And although they are always composed of the same three elements—buildings, pumps, and signs—their appearance and presentation have varied greatly in the continuing drama of gasoline. They're all trying to sell the same thing—a highly volatile, amber-colored liquid—so that any design expression provides the sole product differentiation.

The first were "filling stations," often a pump out front of a drug or feed store; then they became tiny separate buildings. In the 1920s, filling stations evolved into "service stations." Service bays were added; hydraulic lifts replaced pits in the ground. They offered free air and road maps. Attendants donned snazzy uniforms and leather puttees and would offer to wash your car as well as your windshield. And let us remember that great innovation, "the registered rest room," which replaced the "picking-flower stops" that had been the previous necessity. Euphemistically, the gas station provided a "comfort stop" and a "comfort station"—two of the all-time great American ostrich terms. That was in the days of innocence.

Various kinds of gas stations were built: Prefabricated stations began to be built from the teens onward on the West Coast, like the Hubcap Corner in Dishman, Washington (photograph 19). These had a vocabulary of prefabricated elements that were put together to make various configurations for different locations. In the 1930s porcelain enamel panels were introduced. They gleamed in the sun, could be made into colorful compositions, and required no particular maintenance. The public hated the white-and-blue striped tile Gulf stations; they called them "ice boxes." They were replaced with plastics in the 1960s, when porcelain enamel became too expensive.

And gas stations were built in the shape of other objects—representational shapes like windmills, lighthouses, or oil cans, such as the Gallon Measure service station in Buchanan, New York (photograph 51); and even in the shape of dinosaurs, like the former Sinclair station just south of Weeki Wachee Springs, Florida (photograph 91). (A postcard boasts: "The only Dinosaur Station of its kind in the World. Overall length 110 feet; main body 34 feet high; head 48 feet high.")

Gas stations were also built in the traditional historical styles of architecture—colonial, Spanish Mission (photograph 30—the Richfield gas station at Goleta, California), and Art Deco (photograph 25—the Standard Oil gas station). Then there were half-timbered Tudor stations along with English provincial hunting lodges, medieval castles, Indian tepees, and Chinese pagodas (photograph 27—Seneca Mobil)—if you can call these latter traditional architectural styles.

Most idiosyncratic of all were the stations built to commemorate local traditions or historical events: The Bomber station in Milwaukie, Oregon, is a monument to the B17 bomber, and owner Art Lacey propped one of them—all thirty-two tons—up above the pumps "as a memento to the passing era of the propeller driven airplane" (photograph 17). Gas-N-Go (photograph 18) is a flying saucer in Ashtabula, Ohio, circa 1962. And the Hat N' Boots gas station on East Marginal Way near the Boeing plant in Seattle (photograph 20) has its men's and women's toilets in the boots.

The gas pumps themselves reflect the history of technology and design. They are mainly intended to show off with as much theatricality as possible the process of getting the fluid into the tank—and, later, of acting as cash register, as well. First came visible pumps (photographs 5 and 6) that were pumped by hand to draw the gas up into a globe or cylinder at the top where it could be seen—a graduated-beaker kind of arrangement; from there it was gravity-fed into the car tank. Since the gas could be seen, companies tinted it in different colors—Texaco had green gasoline; Standard Oil of New York (SOCONY) had red.

In time those visible pumps were replaced by clockface pumps in which the gas was concealed, except for a little rotating eye or spinner that gave proof positive that something was actually going into the car tank. Then, tall thin refrigerator and short fat refrigerator shapes were developed. Next, as the technology got better and styling kept pace, gas pumps became sleeker, slimmer. Now they are computerized.

But even more important than the station or the pumps were the signs emblazoned with the memorable graphic symbols of our culture. The sign was the first indication of a gas station as you were driving along. National oil companies proclaimed themselves memorably. Gulf first put blue block letters on orange signs in 1922; SOCONY's classic Flying Red Horse made their earlier symbol, a gargoyle, extinct in 1932. Smaller, independent oil companies also came forth with their trademarks—the Citizens 77 greyhound in southwestern Georgia; the Bell bell in the

Southwest. In southeastern Georgia and Florida two competing Colonial Oil companies pitted an eagle against a Minuteman.

Food: Eats

Besides creating frustrated excitement in the minds of children, establishments purveying food and drink sprang up along the road because people had to stop to eat sometime. There was a staggering variety of buildings, all dispensing about the same menu—diners, drive-ins, barbecues, roadhouses. Howard Johnson's, White Towers and White Castles, McDonald's, Kentucky Fried Chicken, and Denny's—these are the evolution of eating places. Basically, they all offer a short-order format that encourages one to keep moving on the road.

Diners that looked like railroad cars suggested that one had not even stopped but was still moving while eating—as if on the train. Despite their appearance, most diners were not reused railroad cars. They were prefabricated buildings produced by major manufacturers specifically for roadside and city use. The Miss Bellows Falls Diner in Vermont (photograph 67) and many like it throughout New England were produced by a company in Worcester, Massachusetts, while the Valentine Diner Company in Kansas spread its units all over the Midwest (photographs 70 and 71).

Many short-order places all over the country presented themselves in buildings shaped like their products or a related shape—chuck wagons, root-beer barrels, oranges (photographs 54 and 55), coffee pots (photograph 50), and even hot-dog-shaped hot-dog stands. And don't forget the milk bottles, milk cans, windmills, and tepees. The Sandy Jug Tavern in Portland, Oregon, started life as an ice cream parlor. Similarly, the Hoot Owl Café near Los Angeles (photograph 73) began as the "Hoot Hoot I Scream." The most spectacular of these "pop architecture" buildings I have found is Mammy's Cupboard in Natchez, Mississippi, on Old Highway 61 (photograph 61), shaped like what her neighbors affectionately call her, "Black Mammy." Mammy opened as a skirt in 1939; her upper extremities were added later—she is carrying a tray and wears horseshoe earrings.

Then there were the simplistic, cartoon-like ethnic images to indicate slightly more exotic fare—Italian, Chinese, and Mexican. Chinese restaurants are a topic unto themselves, their blatant tackiness overwhelming many of the other strip buildings. They have their own architectural vocabulary of weird lettering, dragons, pagodas, and intense colors. The George Joe (photograph 56) in La Mesa, California, is one of my favorites; it appears to be a Chinese-style barn with additions. On the other hand, the Canton Café in Galesburg, Illinois (photograph 65), sticks to the old white-wood clapboard vernacular, its Chineseness divulged by its less than subtle Chinese-red graphics girdling the building. One Chinese restaurant continues to puzzle me; it is the Uranium Café in Grants, New Mexico (photograph 35). Its sign seems to celebrate nearby nuclear tests.

Italian places are only a little more subtle. There is a nationwide epidemic of Leaning Towers of Pizza, and they're impossible to miss. The first one I saw was in Cambridge, Massachusetts, in the early 1960s, but it's no longer there. I've since seen or heard about towers in Green Brook, New Jersey (photograph 57), Saugus, Massachusetts, Chicago, and San Diego. My other favorite pizza image is the leering Jolly Cholly pizza sign in North Attleboro, Massachusetts (photograph 34). Mexican restaurants abound too. The only problem with the trite Mexican atop the Sombrero Taco Shop in San Diego (photograph 63) is that he appears to be awake; most of the other Mexican roadside stereotypes are asleep leaning against a cactus with their sombreros covering their eyes.

Sleep: Grand Motels

Motels are essential to life on the road. Apocryphally, they started as that extra room at a farmer's house along the road. The extra rooms evolved into cabins, much like the bungalow colony form of vacation housing but with the lawn paved over, making them "bungalow courts." Then the individual cabins got joined into continuous units of rooms, and the universal motel form had arrived.

Many of these Kleen and Kozy Kabins (it was a germ-conscious era before penicillin) were spruced up in other ways. One of the establishments claiming to be the first to use the name motel—the Motel Inn, alongside Highway 101 in San Luis Obispo, California (1925)—adopted the persona of a Spanish Mission along the old El Camino Real. Frank Redford patented his design for a Wigwam Village Motel in 1936, when he built his first batch of tepee rooms with a large tepee—office—gas station structure. Redford's chain and others (Wigwam Lodge, TeePee Motel, etc.) sprang up all over the country—romantic, adventurous visions. And the nonsense didn't stop there; there were Alamo Plaza motels (photograph 108), log cabins (photograph 116), farmhouses, you name it.

Part of Frank Redford's chain, the Wigwam Village, Rialto, California, has recently been restored, and they adopted that very up-to-date phrase, "Do It in a Teepee" as their new slogan. This points up an old fact: motels have had a sleazy reputation for most of their existence. J. Edgar Hoover declared them sinful in the late 1930s, and they have been the subject of a thousand salacious jokes: "What is motel spelled backwards?" is one of them.

The most important aspect of motel design has always been what you can see from the road—the sign, the office, and sometimes an unused swimming pool. In the old days, when you were going 35 mph, the neon signs could be finely articulated into forms such as Indians and bellhops (photographs 100 and 101), and you could indulge in nonsense like tepees and Alamos.

The big chains, with their standardized facilities and graphic images, began to evolve as early as 1940 when a group of Southern motel owners got together and founded Quality Courts. The first Holiday Inn was opened in Memphis, Tennessee, in 1953, by a disgruntled motel user, one Kemmons Wilson. He got draftsman Eddie Bluestein to design his sign. Bluestein modeled it after a movie marquee and sketched in the name Holiday Inn at the bottom because he had just seen a rerun of the 1942 Bing Crosby and Fred Astaire movie of that name. That sign made history.

Now the motel room is nearly identical wherever you go: the new International Style in architecture. The difference between a Holiday Inn room and a Ramada room is the difference between a Buick and a Pontiac. Not that much. As a 1975 Holiday Inn commercial intoned, "The best surprise is no surprise." I hate to admit it, but they've got something there. What the buildings and offices look like no longer matters that much; it is the signs that count. From Maine to California, the motel chains try to project an instant, reassuring message of rest and relaxation.

Fun: Roadside Amusements

Seemingly the most unnecessary stop you could ever make, and definitely the places you could never get your parents to stop at (but why, then, are all those cars always parked in front?), are the roadside attractions that looked most exciting of all. Since their purpose is so marginal, entrepreneurs tried all the more to make you stop by an endless series of billboards Burma-shaved across the landscape. The billboards were more important than the buildings themselves; the buildings were usually obscured by hedges or a tall fence blocking the quick lateral view of the highly touted treasures promised within. Exploitative regional and local sideshows and zoos seduce the most gullible travelers into stopping—"See the Dinosaur Bone," "Visit the World's Largest Snake," "Alligators!!!" "Here It Is" and "You Missed It" are the billboards denoting the entrance and exit. What a way to sell.

Gatorland in St. Augustine, Florida; Rock City in Chattanooga, Tennessee; Santa's Land in Putney, Vermont; Reptile Gardens in Rapid City, South Dakota (photograph 94); Burketown in Greensberg, Kansas (photograph 93); and Pioneer Village in Minden, Nebraska—they all make a sideshow of the road. Pay a couple of bucks to see a bunch of zoo animals or a stage-set Main Street; buy some souvenirs; and if we can slip some sugar water into you, we will.

Another type of roadside attraction is the "museum." Gas stations have become frozen in time by being transformed into museums. Charles Ellis moved an old gas station seven miles outside Carthage, Missouri, and has filled it with gas station artifacts (photograph 29); an Art Deco Auburn-Cord automobile showroom and factory in Auburn, Indiana, has become, naturally enough, an automobile museum. Then there are the grandma's attic storefront museums as in Monroe, Oregon (photograph 96), and Cambridge, Idaho (photograph 95). The most absurd of all is the dinosaur "Prehistoric Museum" in the desert outside Palm Springs, California (photograph 90). This huge green monster, next to a café, houses a display and a gift shop.

The eighty-foot-long Wall Drug dinosaur in Wall, South Dakota (photograph 92), is less related to the Cabazon, California, monster than it is to the parking-lot dinosaur at Gatorland. Wall Drug is a drugstore gone amok; it proclaims itself with billboards for hundreds of miles in all directions (one bill lures with "Free Ice Water"—what a deal!). The Wall Drug dinosaur has no function but to stand by the interstate as the ultimate billboard, the irresistible last venal gasp.

Every bit as meretricious as the Wall Drug dinosaur are the gift shops and Indian trading posts that have no attractions except their goods and the sugar water. A New Yorker cartoonist sums it all up perfectly with his drawing of an indistinct building with loads of cars parked in front of the sign, "Larry's Painted Desert Schlock Shop; fake handicrafts; tasteless souvenirs; overpriced gifts; phony junk."

Another roadside amusement, drive-in movies, was much more for adults than for kids. The first one opened in Camden, New Jersey, on May 16, 1932. Drive-in movies are the first indications of civilization. They are located between towns and define their borders. This location serves many purposes: the movie could draw on the populations of two towns; the land was cheaper; and neither town could be held responsible for what was considered a sleazy place. The phenomenon came to house a ritual— where you went to make out in place of a lovers' lane 'cause you couldn't do it at home. There's a drive-in on the border between Panama City and Springfield, Florida, called the "Isle of View" (say it fast). With today's new values and with television, of course nobody needs drive-in movies anymore. So many of them sit dying along the roadside—the Stonehenges of America.

The drive-in movie consists of a huge billboard screen, often with an office or snack bar worked into it, and a huge parking lot. In order to attract attention to their establishments, some owners elaborately decorated the backs of the screens, which faced the road. The all-time drive-in movie cliché imagery—crescent moon and stars—adorns the drive-in in Cape Girardeau, Missouri (photograph 81). Many drive-ins wear their histories on their sleeves—you can tell by the wings on each side of the Keno Family Drive-In, Kenosha, Wisconsin (photograph 79), for example, where the screen increased in size with the change from 16 mm films to 35 mm. The Trail in Amarillo (photograph 88), the Airline in Houston (photograph 80), and the Sunset in Tazwell, Virginia (photograph 76), all show what could be done with a coat of paint, some neon, and a lot of imagination.

The flashiest drive-ins are to be found in California, where at least two companies competed for the creation of elaborate murals on the backs of screens—great public works of art. My favorite was the twin-surfer mural at the Olympic Drive-In in Santa Monica, but that was torn down to make way for a Cadillac dealership—sic transit gloria. Often the murals were accented with neon for nocturnal viewing: witness the spectacular baton twirler at the Campus in San Diego (photograph 89). Others of this genre include the Mission at San Juan Capistrano (photograph 85) and the Tri-City in Loma Linda (photograph 84), with its spectacular depiction of a skier from the nearby San Bernardino Mountains.

The End of the Road: The End

Now, the era of the road may be coming to an end, along with the automobile-related buildings and the culture it engendered. The new life-style of the energy crisis casts a pall over the future of roadside industries. If gasoline shortages turn into gasoline rationing, there are going to be a lot of empty coffee shops and motel rooms out there. How will it all end—or where? It is going to end with the cars sputtering out of gas by the side of the road—not getting to the end of it. It's going to end with all of the places along the road being deserted, turning very quickly into dust and then into nothingness—a sort of paved wilderness where before there was an unpaved wilderness. We are heading into an era in America when we cannot afford to drive anymore—to be mobile and free. We will no longer be able to get in our cars and go out and explore as if we were Christopher Columbuses. It will simply be too expensive and not geared to the time and pace of today.

Already the roadsides are lined with the relics of that adventurous frontier, the remnants that are instant ruins. Already nearly half of the old drive-in movies are blitzed—torn down or decaying. Gas stations are closing at a ferocious rate. The interstates have killed off all of the commerce in the small towns they bypassed. In Kingsland, Georgia, where I-95 has replaced old U.S. 17 within the last few years, there is practically nothing left of the town. And when the interstates are deserted, the new interstate cities will become brand-new ghost towns.

How can we save this architecture? We have to reassess our standards for historic preservation or else all these buildings will be gone before they are old enough to be considered for preservation. People are beginning to see that what looked like trash to them before was not so bad after all—especially in view of what it would cost to recreate. Scholars, historians, and preservationists are taking a closer look. Roadside buildings are finding their way into architectural guidebooks. The National Trust for Historic Preservation has been working to educate merchants to the inherent values of their buildings on Main Street and to teach them that their buildings should be respected rather than destroyed. They are saying, "Take off the layer of the 1950s and 1960s and reveal the original layer of 1920s underneath." And a new organization for the preservation of these kinds of buildings has been formed—the Society for Commercial Archeology. The Modern Diner in Pawtucket, Rhode Island (photograph 66), has become the first diner to be listed on the National Register of Historic Places. Gas stations are making the register as well.

People are also beginning to ask how these roadside buildings could be saved and reused for other purposes in the future. Maybe some could be turned, intact, into Disneyesque villages—Carland, Autoland, roadside attractions. Some reuse has taken place in the normal course of happenstance: one gas station, in Pacoima, California (photograph 26), has been transformed from pumping gas to delivering fundamentalist religion. A house of worship where lube trucks used to be, now the ultimate service station. There are also gas stations that are now used as real estate offices; others have become restaurants and homes. Motels are more difficult to reform. Some have been turned into dormitories and apartments, but more often they are torn down and replaced by shopping centers or car washes.

With most of these buildings, however, there seems to be nothing to do, and they just crumble away. So we must take a long, lasting look at this architecture. It is an important record of our culture and, perhaps, of our dreams. It is something that we share in common. It is a great achievement in American architecture.

1
De Valls Bluff, Ark.

2
Calvary, Ga.
Rt. 111

3
Mountain Grove, Mo.
Mobil Flying Red Horse
Rt. 60B

4
Gulf Breeze, Fla.
Rt. 98

8
Wauneta, Nebr.
Venita St.

9
Buchanan, N.Y.
Rotary Kerosene Pump

10
Fleetville, Pa.
Clockface Pump

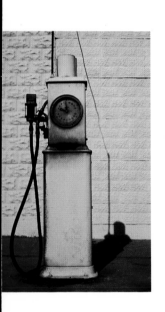

11
Utica, Nebr.

12
Weston, Ohio
Rt. 6

13
Yoder, Kans.
Derby Gas Pumps

14
Sacramento, Calif.
Alhambra Blvd.

15
Windham, N.Y.

16
Barstow, Calif.
Main St.

17
Milwaukie, Ore.
Bomber Gas
Rt. 99E

19
Dishman, Wash.
Hub Cap Corner

20
Seattle, Wash.
Hat N' Boots Gas
E. Marginal Way

23
Phelps, Mo.
Bill's Gas
Rt. 96

24
Creston, Iowa
Bill's Service Station
Rt. 34

27
West Allis, Wisc.

29
Carthage, Mo.
Gas Station Museum
Rt. 96

30
Goleta, Calif.
Richfield Station

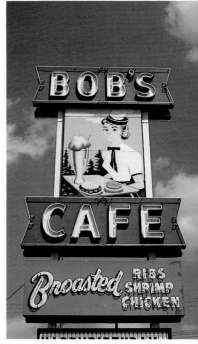

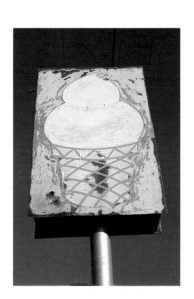

43
Wichita, Kans.

44
Ely, Nev.

45
Pensacola, Fla.

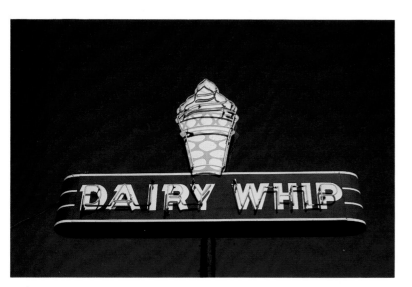

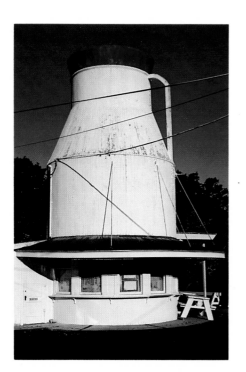

GEORGE JOE

CANTONESE CUISINE

George Joe BANQUET ROOM
Call 469-0158

SUNDAY Open 12 NOON

DINNER FOR TWO $19.50

← PARKING →

60
Sullivan, Wisc.
Bar-B-Q
Rt. 18

61
Natchez, Miss.
Mammy's Cupboard
Rt. 61

62
Amarillo, Tex.
Beer Bar
Rt. 66

63
San Diego, Calif.
Sombrero Taco Shop
El Cajon Blvd.

68
Ellenville, N.Y.
Diner

69
Buellton, Calif.
Dining Cars Café

70
Shawnee, Okla.
Hamburger Castle
Beard St.

98
Allentown, Ariz.
Indian City
I-40

99
Pensacola, Fla.
Rt. 90

100
Blaine, Tenn.
Rt. 11W

107
Lordsburg, N.Mex.
Hightower Motel
Old Rt. 80

108
Memphis, Tenn.
Alamo Plaza Motel
Rt. 70

109
Beaumont, Tex.

110
Idaho Falls, Idaho

111
Bellevue, Wash.

 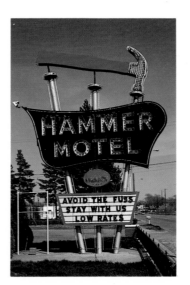 

119
Albuquerque, N.Mex.
Souvenirs Tepee
Rt. 66

120
Sierra Blanca, Tex.
Tepee Rest Area
I-10

121
Allentown, Ariz.
Indian City Exxon Station
I-40

122
Hastings, Nebr.
DLD Motel
Rt. 6

123
Holbrook, Ariz.
Wigwam Motel
Rt. 66

124
Cave City, Ky.
Wigwam Village
Rt. 31W

125
Seattle, Wash.
Twin T.P.'s Restaurant

126
Rockerville, S.Dak.
Horseless Carriage Museum Billboard
Rt. 16